Rise and Shine

Welcome to Busy Book 1!

Find the items hidden in the book.

The Busy Book helps children develop in the following areas of learning…

 **Communication**
Learning to speak together in English.

 **Movement**
Being active and building confidence.

 **Finding out**
Learning about and exploring the world.

 **Critical thinking**
Solving problems and puzzles and learning thinking skills.

 **Creativity**
Expressing ideas through drawing and making.

 **We can do it!**
Celebrating learning and progress.

1 Old toys, new toys

Find

Look and trace.

tablet 3 or 1
balls 4 or 5
cars 2 or 6
dolls 2 or 3

The talking toy

Play with me, play with me, please can you play with me?
The car is big, the train is small, the teddy bear is old.
I'm nice and new, looking at you.

color me

The robot is new.
The car is big.

Let's create

What is it?

It's a house.

It's a robot.

It's a rocket.

Draw your idea here!

 Say with me!

 one  red  rocket

 two  blue  robots

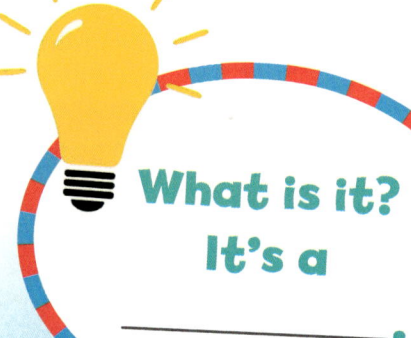
What is it? It's a _____.

Explore with Grandma Belinda
Our world

What toys can you find at home?

An old toy

A new toy

A yellow toy

A small toy

A big toy

Ask your family
What's your favorite toy?

Grandma Belinda's Fun Facts

This is a *puppet*.

Make and act

Find what you need

1. Think and choose your toy.

2. Plan and draw.

3. Make your toy.

I'm a robot.

I'm a ball.

Imagine you are your toy. Act with friends.

All kinds of families

Spot the difference.

How many differences can you find?

8 5 10

Match

uncle   grandma   mom   brother

Explore with Grandma Belinda — Our world

Who can you see?

- In my story book
- On TV
- On my street

- mom
- dad
- sister
- brother
- grandma
- grandpa
- auntie
- uncle
- cat
- fish
- bird

Ask your family
Do you have a pet?

Grandma Belinda's Fun Facts

A baby cat is a kitten.

Make and mime

Find what you need

1 Think and plan your stick family.

2 Make your stick family.

3 Play and say.

This is my brother.

What sound does your pet make?

What am I?

A cat!

Mime a pet and guess.

3 Amazing bodies

Find the body parts.

hand

arm

leg

feet

Look and trace

eyes 2 or 5
nose 1 or 3
ears 2 or 4
mouth 1 or 6

Who am I?

I have four legs, I have big ears, and brown eyes.

Who am I? I'm a _____.

I have a small mouth and two blue eyes.

Who am I?

I'm a _____.

I have two small ears and a big nose. **Who am I?**

I'm a _____.

Let's talk

Complete and say.

I can...	Me	My friend
run	✓ ✗	✓ ✗
dance	✓ ✗	✓ ✗
jump	✓ ✗	✓ ✗
hop	✓ ✗	✓ ✗

I can run.

Me, too!

How many body parts can you name?

Explore with Grandma Belinda — Our world

What can we do?

My friend can...

I can...

My teacher can...

My dad can...

My mom can...

Grandma Belinda's Fun Facts

Ask your family
Can you jump rope?

The girl can jump rope.

Make and say

Find what you need

1 Think and plan your puppet.

2 Make your puppet.

3 Play and say.

I can sing.

I have two ears and four legs.

Draw a pet.

Remember! Give your pet:
- eyes
- nose
- feet
- legs
- mouth
- ears

Talk about your pet with a friend.

Make and do

Find what you need

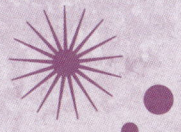

1 Think and choose four foods.

2 Draw and cut.

3 Make your food mobile.

Try a new food.

It's a _____. I like it.

I don't like it.

Draw it, smell it, touch it, eat it.

Let's create

Describe with a friend.

Is it a butterfly and a duck?

No, it isn't.

Is it a mouse and a butterfly?

Yes, it is.

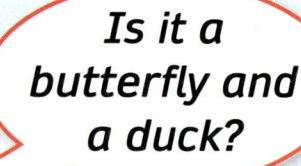

Create a new animal.

Say with me!

Four frogs, five flowers.

Describe your new animal to a friend.

Make and do

Find what you need

1. Think and choose your animal.

2. Plan and draw.

3. Make your animal.

 What animals can you hear outside?

Go on a sound hunt.

Let's dress up

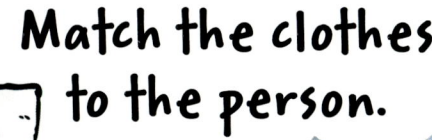

Match the clothes to the person.

What is he wearing?

I'm wearing my _____ and _____.

Let's talk

I'm wearing my...		My friend
jeans	✓	✓
boots	✓	✓
skirt	✓	✓
hat	✓	✓
T-shirt	✓	✓
pants	✓	✓
sweater	✓	✓
shorts	✓	✓
shoes	✓	✓
dress	✓	✓

Ask your friend!

Are you wearing a sweater?

Yes, I am. It's red.

Say something nice about your friend's clothes.

I like your T-shirt!

Thank you!

Say with me!

T-shirt, skirt, socks, and shoes.

Explore with Grandma Belinda
Our world

What different clothes do you wear?

At home

At school

When it's cold

When it's hot

My favorite clothes

Ask your family
What are your favorite clothes?

Grandma Belinda's Fun Facts

This is a coat.

Make and act

1 Think and choose your clothes.

2 Plan and draw.

3 Make your clothes.

Find what you need

Choose a character from a book, a movie, or Rise and Shine!

Look! I'm Elena, I'm wearing a red sweater.

Dress up as your favorite character and act.

I'm Dexter. I'm wearing blue jeans.

Rise and Shine Goodbye

Rise and Shine Certificate

You finished the book!
Great work!

Awarded to: _____   Age: _____

Dexter	Elena	Bruno	Grandma Belinda	Kiki
Dexter	Elena	Bruno	Grandma Belinda